LIFTING THE LATCH

FRANK DULLAGHAN

CinnamonPress

INDEPENDENT INNOVATIVE INTERNATIONAL

Published by Cinnamon Press
Meirion House
Tanygrisiau
Blaenau Ffestiniog
Gwynedd, LL41 3SU
www.cinnamonpress.com

The right of Frank Dullaghan to be identified as author of this work has been asserted by him in accordance with the Copyright, Designs and Patent Act, 1988. Copyright © 2018 Frank Dullaghan. ISBN: 978-1-78864-011-4

British Library Cataloguing in Publication Data. A CIP record for this book can be obtained from the British Library.

Designed and typeset in Palatino by Cinnamon Press. Printed in Poland.

Cover design by Adam Craig from original artwork: 'Lifting the Latch' by Aidan Dullaghan, © used with thanks.

Cinnamon Press is represented in the UK by Inpress Ltd and in Wales by the Welsh Books Council.

Acknowledgements

These poems or earlier versions of them have been published in the following places: *Coast to Coast to Coast* (UK); *Causeways* (UK); *Dubai Irish Society Yearbook 2017* (UAE); *Frogmore Papers* (UK); *Galway Review* (Ire); *High Window* (UK); *Ink, Sweat, and Tears* (UK); *London Grip* (UK); *Nimrod* (US); *Paris Lit Up* (Fra); *Ponder Review* (US); *Queen's Quarterly* (Can); *Rattle Respond* (US); *The Stare's Nest* (UK); *Sukoon* (Leb).

Hands took 2nd place in the Origami Poems Project Competition and was published in their *Kindness* anthology (US) 2017. *Things I Don't Know* was accepted for publication in an anthology of refugee poems by Eyewear Publishing 2015. *There is Nowhere Left* was accepted for publication in the anthology *Making Mirrors* 2016. *The Children Are Silent* was nominated for Best on the Net in 2016 A selection of these poems were Highly Commented in the Munster Literature Centre's Fools for Poetry international chapbook competition.

I'd like to thank Hind Shufani and Zeina Hashem Beck for providing platforms where some of these poems were first performed. Thanks is also due to Ann Drysdale and to Zeina Hashem Beck for their close reading of these poems. My son Aidan has once again supplied the cover artwork and my wife, Marie, as usual, endured my recital of first drafts of many of these. So a big thanks to them also.

Frank Dullaghan holds an MA with Distinction in Writing (University of South Wales). He co-founded the *Essex Poetry Festival* in the UK and is a previous editor of *Seam Poetry Magazine* He has published three previous collections from Cinnamon Press (*On the Back of the Wind*, 2008; *Enough Light to See the Dark*, 2011; *The Same Roads Back*, 2014) and two haiku collections. He has been a children's poetry judge for the Emirates Airline Festival of Literature since 2013. In 2014 he was commissioned to provide the final English translation of HH Sheikh Mohammed's poetry, published as *Flashes of Verse*. In 2016, he published a pamphlet, *Secrets of the Body*, a sequence of poems on the life of Pope Joan, with Eyeware Publications. He has lived in Dubai since 2006.

Contents

Small Town Brewery Blues:

The Mouth Organ	11
The Best of Days	12
The Piano	13
The Day of the Robin	14
On the Way to School	15
Doing the Deed	16
The Fathers	17
Worship	18
The Ramparts	19
Small Town Brewery Blues	20
How the Mind Works	21
No Use Blaming the Choices We Make on the Dead	22
Knee Job	23
My Mother Held Back Time	25
Holding Your Tongue	26

The Children Are Silent:

On Not Liking Pastoral Poems	29
Gaza Haiku	30
A Liberation	31
Gaza i. Rooms	32
ii. School	
iii. Doll	
iv. Stories	
Days of Blindness Now	34
Let the Mountains Hold On	35
Things I Don't Know	36
There is Nowhere Left	38
The Children are Silent	39
Daughter	40
Promenade des Anglais	41
Love Poem	42
She Opens the Small Glass Door	43
Only the Rain	44

Aisling:

Aisling: Beirut	47
Under the Table	49

Now That It's Happened   51
Last Confession   52
That Young One   53

    i. That Young One Has a Strange Head
    ii. That Young One Always Leaves the Road
    iii. The Dark Father Asks a Question
    iv. That Young One Finds a Way
    v. One Morning She Witnesses the Bright Father
    vi. That Young One Worries She'll Forget
    v. She Sees the Bright Mother Crying
    vi. The Dark Father Tells a Story
    vii. That Young One Watches the Dark Mother
    viii. There Are Blue Lights Flashing
    ix. Are You Looking for Me?
    x. That Young One is Sweeping the Floor

Lazarus Leaving:

Lazarus Leaving   63
Digging   64
Jinn   65
All Souls' Night   66
The Voices of the Dead   67
Words are Less than Half the Story   68
Late into London Blues   70
The North   71
Dancing with the Dead   72
Wind 74

Beannacht:

Prayer for Ramadan   77
Love Poem for Oreo   78
Apple   81
Weight   82
Night after Night   83
Remembering Your Green Dress   84
At the Gym   86
Hands   87
Ghazal: Marie   88
Beannacht   89

Notes   90

*For my Son Aidan and his wife Louise,
married 3 April 2018*

Lifting the Latch

Small Town Brewery Blues

The Mouth Organ

Dundalk, 1964

I showed her how to build a house
with Lego bricks, the red roof tiles turning
on an L-shaped plan, a dormer window,

like the bungalow she could see
from the window of our small front bedroom.
She taught me how to knit.

She was bed-ridden. My mother took her in
when her own relatives hesitated, grown too
loose in their lives for the sudden tightening

of that responsibility. Two young women and
their mother visited infrequently. They called her
Aunty too, which I suppose she was.

They were there at the end when I
was sent outside to wheeze and blare
notes at the sky from my new mouth organ.

When they came out to tell me,
I laughed out loud at their hysterics.
But I flung the mouth organ far

into the long back garden's grass
when the word *gone* sank in, stood there
under that cloud-heavy sky emptied of song.

The Best of Days

Her brothers came with bags of food
and stood at her half-opened door.
She widened it to let them in.
They filled the kitchen, refused
the offered chairs, the tea.
Their resentment bulked them
like itinerants dressed in multiple overcoats.
The conversation was always the same:
there was work to be had
if my father *just got up off his arse,*
if he got on his bike, did
what any other man would do.
My mother always remained silent
until they ran out of anger,
mumbled into that silence and left.
Then one day she said *Stop*,
went to the table, gathered the bags
and placed them back into their arms,
told them that if they had nothing
good to say about her husband
they need not come back.
It took a while but they returned
with their bags of food and a dark
plug of pipe tobacco for my father.
It made my mother cry. Later she smiled,
sitting quiet on the back step
as my father strolled in the dark,
the almost forgotten smell of his pipe smoke
seeking her out as if these were
the best of days and should be enjoyed.

The Piano

Dundalk 1960's

Unless its upper lip was closed
it snarled, its white teeth frightening
in the parlour's dark.

Mammy sometimes soothed it,
translating sheet music into song.
Daddy played by ear.

My uncle played honky tonk,
heavy plonking black keys only.
His playing was the worst

but I liked it best—a rough and ready
excitement that seemed forbidden.
Daddy didn't like him much:

mammy's younger brother who,
over the course of a week, laid
a concrete path along the side

of our end of terrace house.
Of course, daddy found the flaws.
But mammy said it was better

than ten year's worth of promises.
As time went by they played less and less.
My uncle didn't call so often.

As I grew up, my fear of it - that sense
of torqued shadow - shrank,
the way all those days grew thin.

The Day of the Robin

Dundalk 1966

I grew to understand it often rained
inside my father's head, that sometimes
he went under, drowned.

But that day he put out his hand
and the robin came to him, a small flutter
of surprise from the close bush.

It perched on the ends of his fingers,
tilted its head one way, then the other,
gave us each eye. My father smiled like a child.

Then with a little ruffle, it pecked
at whatever he held in the plate
of his palm. He had been trying

to coax the bird to him for weeks.
Now that it happened, it seemed so easy,
as if a silent note had been sung in the air.

Even when it finished stabbing
at the food, it was in no hurry to leave,
turning about on his hand in a slow dance.

For a moment, I thought it might settle
down and sleep, the way I'd seen a frog do once
as my father stroked the fat wedge of its head.

He didn't dare his second hand
with the robin but left the air open.
Then it seemed to nod at him, turned, and

hopping up into its opening wings, it circled
above him and flew away. We stood watching
its absence together under the wet sun.

On the Way to School

Dundalk 1967

The brown mare stood huffing and grunting
into the cold air behind the five bar gate.

I stopped and saw a slither of steaming flesh slip
from her, a wet mess on the concrete that tried to stand,

its feet splaying and buckling. I ran to the farmhouse.
I could smell the hot tea on the farmer's breath

as he reached for his cap. *All fucking night and she drops
it now. Did the foal move? It was under the mother*, I said.

Suckling? he asked. I didn't know what that meant
but by then we were there and I could see that it was.

I was late for school but I had a new word, a good word,
to hold against the hunger of those days.

Doing the Deed

Dundalk , 1967

I was almost twelve, she was eleven.
But her sister was fifteen, a woman, and
chaperoned us. Her friends had set it up.
I was following a script
I'd rehearsed for days in my head.
It was late afternoon, the park just beginning
to lose itself in shadow, winter nipping
at the bud of spring. I shivered. Still,
I held her hand. Daffodils crowded the trees.
Birds seemed overly raucous as they settled
into branches. My tongue stumbled
heavy-booted in my mouth. We stepped
into the bandstand, stood behind a post.
Even that young, I knew that this was
the kissing part. Her sister sat on a bench
some way away but I felt we were
being watched from underneath that fringe.
When I leaned in close to whisper
we should move someplace else,
something in her was triggered, some waiting
impulse tilted her face up, closed tight
her eyes. I kissed her mouth.
She kissed me back, a small hard-puckered,
close-mouthed, kiss. So that's it, I thought,
disappointed. But when I stepped back
and watched her eyelids lift, saw
that sudden brightness fill her eyes, the smile
that burst across her face, I needed
to stand close again. But she broke free,
ran to her standing sister—*I did it,*
I did it, did you see!—and was hugged.
Without another word they walked away,
curled around their conversation,
leaving me with a need
to hug myself, wonder what had happened.

The Fathers

Dundalk, 1968

My schoolmates' fathers were stern men
I saw in suits on Sundays. I knew
which ones used the belt, which drank,

and that the small man often battered
his wife. They were to be avoided.
I would see them coming home from work,

stepping off a bus, a bicycle. I felt
they commanded the world, that they
knew what's what about everything.

My own father seemed as lost to them as I,
he kept himself to himself, never
in the pub or at a match. There was nothing

he could say that would make him one of them.
I also knew that if the world began to crack,
it would not be to my own father

I would turn for help, nor to the small man,
who I saw sporting two black eyes
the day his eldest son left for the States.

Worship

Dundalk 1969

I spread a blanket over grass—
the older girl next door
wanting company.
She always wore short skirts,
her pale legs perfect.

Her friend joined us later
to lie in the late sun.
I'd never shared such space before—
two girls who seemed to own
themselves completely.

The friend had darker skin,
wore gypsy clothes,
her hair a frazzle of dark copper.
I remember being enthralled
by her freckles,

the curved shadows
in the vee of her blouse.
She laughed, noticing my attention,
and leaning forward,
opened two more buttons.

Then she growled at me
from the back of her throat.
Something in me awoke.
Knowing it as a call to worship
I tilted my head to the floor.

The Ramparts

Dundalk, 1970

I lounged in against the wall
of an underground club
on the Ramparts, bass notes
booming my bones, Phil Linnet
playing live before he was known.

I had practised for weeks with cigarettes.
I was supposed to be at the Derryhale—
a showband, priests on the watch.
Here even the girls were hard, wore
leather, might blacken your eye.

All summer I shaved my bare chin,
kept *Old Spice* under the mattress.
Mostly I watched or, having gathered
the courage to approach the most lost
looking girl, was told to fuck off.

Once though, I shifted a black-haired girl
two years older than myself. I had not
allowed for the possibility, had
no idea what to do when we stopped
at her doorstep, her front door dark,

the house and terrace asleep.
I must have been a great disappointment.
But she kept me around for a while,
even rubbed my chin, said yes, she could
definitely feel the stubble.

Small Town Brewery Blues

Dundalk, 1973

It was down a wet alley between some shops,
each morning that summer between the shops,
I walked through its sloppy yard; the smell of hops.

I took bottles off a line, placed them in a crate,
warm bottles of local beer, twelve to a crate,
earning money for uni, from morning 'till late.

Most lads left school for the production line,
walked out of school to a production line,
money in the pocket, a life of grime.

Stayed where they started, brought good money home.
Raised a family with the money brought home.
Hard working men gave an edge to the town.

When stacking the crates, a bottle could explode.
Glass glittered the air when a bottle would explode.
One lad lost an eye as he stacked his load.

They gave the dangerous work to casual labour,
jobs no one wanted, done by casual labour.
We needed the money, were employed by the hour.

Kept my face turned away when I built my stack,
blindly crashed crates together constructing my stack,
never complained, took the glass on my back.

When summer was over I left that town,
put my books in a bag and left that town.
I kept the boots they lent me and moved on.
Understood now how hard work makes the man.

How the Mind Works

For Peter—Dundalk 1973

My mother asked if we thought he sounded strange.
My father said no, he sounded fine. I wanted to say
the same. But he did seem strange, released almost,

his mind leaping about like a puppy. An uncle made
the appointment and I stayed home to walk him
the three miles to the hospital. I found it hard

to keep him focused, to keep him to the footpath.
(They say madness make you strong.) *Which Doctor?*
the receptionist asked. *Witch Doctor*, Peter replied

and danced. They kept him in. In the weeks that
followed, they introduced him to electricity. I imagined
his mind lit up like a city, expected him to come home

bright. But he came home beaten, as if carrying
a weight of dark he'd rather not have known.
He kept his mind to himself after that.

No Use Blaming the Choices We Make
on the Dead

Dundalk 1973

Your dead may travel with you but they don't interfere.
They had their chance to fuck up once. You should
have yours. Only your grandmother, maybe, if you ask enough
times, will listen. Mostly though, you get yourself out
of your own messes and try not to let anyone know.
When my first serious girlfriend left me after three teenage years
of being the man, growing into the man, I wanted her back,
I wanted her to get over the excitement of a boy with a motorbike.
I wanted her to see where I was going with my books,
my leave-this-town beliefs. When that Halloween party broke,
in that sudden surprising way it always did, to play chase
and kiss, she ran into the street in that scatter of girls,
her new boyfriend out of town, and, as the girls peeled off,
she took her own direction. Were the dead watching?
I joined in the chase, following first the main group, then her
best friend, who slowed into a wall shadow as I caught up,
opened her arms to me, kissed me deeply, sweetly. And Mary,
coming back to where the action was, slowed seeing us,
then turned away as if she could hear the dead chuckling.
Whatever chance I might have had was too gone by then
even for a grandmother and her entourage to fix,

Knee Job

Dundalk 1974

He started calling on my mother
when I wasn't there —
a tea break and a chat
on his way north through Dundalk.
He had picked me up a few times
when I hitched home from Uni.
The Troubles were happening over the border
and my mother worried
I'd brought it indoors and,
with my father working in Dublin, her
without a man in the house all week.
The man seemed a little spaced out
on Prozac — needed a friendly place to stop.
My mother said it could be that
or it could be he might have need
of a safe house and was setting one up.
He was unlikely to be one of the *Boys*,
so most likely one of *the other crowd.*
Back in the day, my grandfather fought
for the Irish Volunteers so perhaps my mother
knew a thing or two. I was charged
with dissuading the man
from dropping in. None of it felt real.
The South suffered a self-inflicted innocence.

But you can never stay immune.
Another man drinking whiskey from the bottle,
when I went in for my night shift as a barman
that summer, was left to himself,
the bottle on the house.
I was told he wasn't there.
I was told the same again
when they came and took him into the jacks.

I can still hear the bang of the gun
and the scream. *Youse have seen nothin'.*
The manager called an ambulance.
It's alright, he told me, *just one of the Boys*
who wanted out. A knee job.
He sent me home early that night,
said I was no use to him
if I couldn't pull a steady pint.

My Mother Held Back Time

Birmingham 1984

Her voice spooled through my Birmingham
living room, a place she'd never been.
Only once had she crossed the water
out of Ireland—a bus trip to Lourdes with neighbours.
Her heart beginning to give up on her,
prayer seemed a better option than the knife.

Her Dundalk accent snagged me,
years away as I was from that place, that time,
my ear moderated, like my tongue, away from its roots.
She returned from Lourdes breathless,
was given a date by her doctor—the Mater Hospital, Dublin.
I was gone by then, married, was *not to be disturbed*.

But that day, later, in Birmingham when I closed
my eyes, she was there with me, laughing,
bustling between the white sink in the scullery
and the range, her pots ready to chuckle to themselves
when she slapped them onto the hot plate,
the commotion and noise a kind of love.

This was the same kitchen
she'd come home to after her operation. Fighting
her pain she had stood by the side of her bed and smiled
when the doctor did his rounds; gained her release.
It was the same kitchen in which she then sat immobile
in her armchair, the room dimming, no longer hers,

my sisters minding her; the kitchen where
her heart leapt from its stitches and stopped her. And now
there was that same kitchen in my Birmingham living room—
its heavy table, its sideboard where my father hid
his miniature bottles of whiskey, a statue of the Virgin
on a shelf, and my mother forever moving about.

Holding Your Tongue

For Fergus

A stick on a cord about the neck,
notched by the teacher for every word they spoke

in their own tongue, taken home
for another beating there, to keep them

on the straight, if cruel, road out
from their potato patch. There's no doubt

that my ancestors were complicit. I had no time
for that knurled, befuddled, crime

but had no interest either, no ability nor inclination
to participate in the language's reintroduction

though the De la Salle brothers had that same trick
of trying to beat a language into boys, the same knack

of being on the moral low ground.
But pain works only in the short term, I've found:

I never kept it up. *Mo ghrá gheal.*
A ghrá mo chroi. But it's a different tale

for my Great Britain born son,
his shelf full of Gaelic books, *Dineen,*

weeks in the *Gaeltacht,* his English tongue
turning milk into buttermilk, as if on the first rung

of a climb back to that potato patch,
as if home again to that *tigín,* lifting the latch.

The Children are Silent

On Not Liking Pastoral Poems

For Hind

Even the daffodils bugling in the spring,
that symbol of renewal, of a fresh start,
the greener grass expected on the other side
of destruction, of bulldozed homes;
even the remnants of the great forests,
fervently pushing out their mossed barks,
girding themselves in stoutness, aren't enough.
You say you cannot accept the pastoral
in poems when what's needed is skin,
tough or otherwise, the way it carries us,
fragile bundles that we are; confused,
jumbled and terrorised as we are,
from one atrocity to the next, from
one scourging of the heart to the next.
You have no time in poems, for the soft
slapping of sea, the chirping of named birds
or the messages they carry like feathers
to a nest. In these days of destitution
you want to clasp hands with people in poems,
you want them to be gifted that much life.

Gaza Haiku

who sees
the sunlight that falls
after the bombs?

your home
will not be your home—
they come with their guns

a child
with her brains gone—
still the bombs fall

a *knock on the door*—
you leave everything behind
go with your life

hospitals are full—
still they come
bearing their bodies

children are moved
from one place of worry
to another

self-defense—
a cat's excuse
to a mouse

politicians
argue
the body count

A Liberation

This shell, it turned out, landed smack in the middle of the Jabaliya cemetery
Josh Glancy reporting on Gaza in The Sunday Times, (UK) 27.07.14

I don't suppose it was any trouble
to them, leaping into the sky like that,
smithereened, baring their bits
to the blasted air. Of course, they came

crashing back to earth, scattered, mixed-
up, not knowing who was who.
But for that while, they were high.
It must have felt like the End of Days,

the Ascension, come upon them,
dancing together, all tooth and grin,
their bones blown towards heaven,
the first to be liberated from Gaza.

But just as quickly as they were lifted,
they were let down—isn't that
how it always is?—their internment
heaped upon them again.

Gaza

The Palestinian fatality toll is 2,131, of whom 1,473 have been identified as civilians, including 501 children, according to preliminary assessments.

UN, OCHA: Occupied Palestinian Territory:
Gaza Emergency Situation Report (as of 4 September 2014, 08:00 hrs)

i. Rooms

She heaves their mattress,
their bedding, through the door,
lodges it against the buttress
of the chimney-breast, the stone
wall, then lets them sleep again,
covers them with prayer.
She steps to the grey window,
calculating the direction of a strike
by noise, instinct, fear.
She will move them again,
will shove them into another room,
if she decides it's safer.
She'll do what she must, be a blanket
herself when the bombs come.

ii. School

The girl's whole family, even her neighbours,
are now at her school—this known place
with blackboards, cupboards,
a UN flag.
          Yet this is where the wall erupts,
where her father blinds her a second
as he flashes red, where her mother crumples
like a spilling bag of rice.
          There is nothing more
she can learn here.

:
)

iii. Doll

She wraps a bandage
around the doll's eyes
so it cannot see, covers its ears
to grant it passage to a new world
of silence. Then she pulls off
both of its legs, yanking them
from their plastic sockets, discovering
how cleanly it happens, the lack
of blood.

iv. Stories

These are the skills they learn:
to take a cable from a building with power,
snake it through rubble to this cellar
to have a working fridge, light.
Thirty-five here each night, climbing
back into themselves, mothers telling

old folktales to their children
as if these evenings are like any other;
fathers telling each other that bombs
never fall in the same place twice,
as if this were true. Open sky
risked for food.

All their dreams travel into the past.
They lay out their small portion
for the morning. If they wake
they will eat it.

Days of Blindness Now

I've been scarred:
a cut from my right temple
to my cheek,
a branch of which scoops
under my right eye,
like I've been glassed.

I got it this morning
around seven-thirty.
I've carried it with me all day
and no one has noticed.
Not my wife. Not my son.
The hands of the girl

who did it were soft.
It was for a movie shoot,
a morning's work.
Even when visible, we don't see
what burdens others carry.
Perhaps our days have grown

too noisy now, too many
voices in the head, too many tasks
tugging at the sleeve, so that even
when we slow all we have left
is the blanket of our weariness,
the need to close our eyes.

Let the Mountains Hold On

For Z

Come whisper your poem in the dark late air.
I'll hold the phone close. I'll close soft the door.
I'll listen minutely (I'll say if it's fine).
Your voice is a cure; your voice is the rain.
       Let the mountains hold on to their silence.

People gather at borders, their families in ruins.
The dead go on living, the living lie down.
Nothing gets fixed (the soiled, the maimed).
But your voice is a balm so I step out of time.
       Let the mountains hold on to their silence.

Everything's slipping. The ice fields flow.
Power is the answer we've learned and we know.
Greed is the agent that never gets turned.
I enter your voice (my cover is blown).
       Let the mountains hold on to their silence.

I have nothing to say that's not been said before.
Your poem is a song. I'm learning the score.
The fuse has been lit (a wing and a prayer).
I'm caught up in your song—oh take your voice lower.
       Let the mountains hold on to their silence.

The children grow up with hate in the food
their mothers spoon-feed them (what's bad becomes good).
They are waiting to kill: their god is their fuel.
But your poem is the only flag I'll unfurl.
       Let the mountains hold on to their silence.

Things I Don't Know

September 2015

I know about lines and forms and desks,
the British invented those.
But I have never queued for salvation, never prayed
not to be sent home.

I know of home, of my own country -
green fields, green welcomes.
But I know nothing of the way hate cocks its gun; that assumed
entitlement to rape; death falling from the sky.

I know of the sky, the boat of it sailing daily.
But I know nothing of how each moment is a spinning barrel,
the chances of dying being greater
than the chances of life.

I know about life, its small inconveniences.
But I know nothing about better-to-risk-it-all-
than-to-stay desperation.
I know nothing about boats.

I know about boats. But not like that,
not recklessly, not as small heavy bobbings overladen
in the crash of a soul-sick sea,
not that deadly form of travel.

I know about travel—motorways, traffic-jams,
airport security checks. But I know nothing about
the pregnant belly of a truck, nothing
about gasping for delivery, for foreign air.

I know about air, its taken-for-granted ease,
like words of belonging. But I know nothing about exile,
nothing about a door closing behind me,
a door closing in front.

I know about front, about getting away with it,
chancing my arm. But I know nothing about facing up,
nothing about seeing the value of my family reduced
to small change in my fists.

I know about fists, the way some people wave them,
the way some say *not our jobs,*
not our benefits, a government that says,
not our problem, not here.

There is Nowhere Left

We move through your borders,
your villages, your countryside.
We walk with our lives
on our backs, our children,
drunk from walking, by the hand,
our pasts blown up behind us.

We move through your language,
your donated food, your fields
of tents. We walk without hope,
as if this is our new reason for being—
this great walk, this achievement
of pushing the miles behind us.

We move through your culture,
your story telling, your politics.
We walk against the turn
of the earth - East to West, our
great numbers slowing its rotation.
We will move through your memories,

your imagination, your knowledge
of yourselves. Our footsteps
will dog the rhythm of your days.
We will walk across your clean
bed linen, your tablecloths, your
conversations. There is no stopping

now that we have started. There is
no use erecting barriers, arguments,
prayers, for you too are moving,
you too are losing your place.

The Children are Silent

The children have learned to be silent.
Their eyes are older than their faces.
They carry their small bodies like suitcases
that they can pick up or put down.

They think their mothers are great engines
that can go on and on,
mile after mile, as if each day
is just another road, as if insanity
can be out-walked.

Their fathers follow like blown sand,
their cupped hands reddening
as they pull the small hope
of cigarette smoke into their lungs.

The children may never speak again.
They have gone beyond words,
grown beyond hope. They know that
all the leaders just sit at the same dark tables
and look at each other.

Daughter

When a bomb un-housed us,
I gave what money I had
to a man with a boat.

Her life will be large in Germany, he said.
My sister will keep to her side.
My travel must wait until there is more money.

This chance was my daughter-gift.
I sent her into the dark,
watched the bob of the boat become water.

She fell off the edge
of my heart. I go each day to the sea,
watch in vain for a note from her future.

Sometimes I go down at night
when the far shore is closer.
My neighbour's child was taken by soldiers.

We live now on broken streets.
My daughter is becoming a woman.
At night, I can feel her

looking over her shoulder.
I went with the chance of a chance
when I sent her. There are no gifts left

that do not hold a hurt.
Daughter, do not look back.
I sent her to the dark of the far shore

from this place of death.
I gave her to the living world,
paid the ferryman.

Promenade des Anglais

Nice, 14 July 2016

Anything can become a weapon —
an airplane, a truck,
the tongue
the thought that proceeds
any of these. A gun.
You have no place to go
when this is over.
There is seldom an end
in sight, death
is more often an ambush.

But when it is visited on us
like this, when it mows us down,
a false answer
to someone else's question,
when it enters us
with hate, insanity,
perhaps we should ban all weapons,
let no one own a gun
or drive a truck,
let no aircraft leave the ground,
have all tongues silenced,
all thoughts hidden under a blanket
of drugs.

Or we could choose
to take our chances, hold hands
and walk the Promenade des Anglais,
watch the sea explode
onto the land,
our backs to the road,
our hearts out there climbing
into the sky,
for the time that we have,
the love we have borrowed.

Love Poem

After Priscila Uppal's 'No Angel in this Death Poem'

There will be no mention of god in this love poem.
The door to heaven is never the one you are pushing
against, but the one you've already entered.

There'll be no mention of doors in this love poem
for people are too busy locking themselves into rooms,
hanging tribal names on them, no-entry signs.

There will be no mention of signs in this love poem.
Portents and prophesies will always let you down. Death
will come seeking you despite your charms.

There will be no mention of death in this love poem
for death is preoccupied with our never ending wars,
his shoulder shattered by the constant recoil of his gun.

There will be no mention of guns in this love poem.
The young are already armed and not planning on growing
old. Cities no longer house music and dance.

There will be no mention of music in this love poem,
no mention of dance. Neither will it mention love.
for this, as you can see, is not a love poem.

She Opens the Small Glass Door

She opens the small glass door
of the carriage clock on her mantelpiece
and snaps the hands off its face.
She takes both of her calendars—
the one on her desk, the magnetic one
on her fridge, and bins them.

Her *iPhone*, she plops like a wish
into the well of the wastepaper basket.
Time will continue but she will not
participate: the sun on her window
in the morning, the lack of it at night, will be
enough. There will be the seasons.

She unplugs the TV and turns it
to face the wall. Her laptop she locks
in an eternal embrace with itself,
super-gluing keyboard to screen.
But the world she will keep
at a safe distance. Outside. Out there,

where other people find their own way
to fight for their lives.

Only the Rain

It's like that half stumbled step
I took onto a stopped travelator,
like confusing the devil
on my left shoulder with the angel
on my right. Like knowing
by heart the wrong things and
never learning what is good for me.

It's like the way only rain
can make me listen to the world—
all of it happening at the same time;
the way thunder can lull me
to sleep, close me into a drawer
of dreams. Like when I know
I'm dreaming but the dream

won't let me out,
as if my heart is not yet ready
for the day. How can we live
with ourselves when we know
so much about the world?
It's as if someone I love has gone
horribly wrong. It's like believing

so easily, holding on too long.
The idea that goodness will win,
like a soap powder ad
of how bright life can be.
It will never come clean.
Still I want to believe. I'm an *amadán*.
It's like I'd never been born.

Aisling

Aisling: Beirut

We are walking down Bliss Street.
Foliage spills through the railings
of AUB. *What will I do,* she asks me,
with my blue leg. Across the street,
a book shop, a café; the road
slow. Posters peel from walls.
> Sometimes the heart is old,
> sometimes it is young.

She is worried it will get stolen.
You must tell me where it will be safe?
We walk within sight of the sea.
High buildings watch the day dip
into the water. I grew up in rain-
drenched Dundalk. I have no answer.
> Sometimes the heart is starlight,
> sometimes it's the sun.

When I was a boy I used to fly.
I would take long skipping steps
until I could bound into air,
soar over roofs. *You must carry it
with you,* I say. There are scooters
parked next to the yellow-topped bollards.
> Sometimes love's spilling over,
> sometimes it's just begun.

There are students out on balconies,
mobile phones to their ears,
some are smoking. There is a helicopter
hovering high. *Will I ever be free
of this leg?* The chopper moves in slow circles,
like longing, refuses to land.
> Sometimes love is whispered,
> sometimes it's a song.

But Dundalk too bordered trouble.
There are places and times too
dream-heavy. Even when gone
they pull you back. *We must walk on,* I say,
night will take the weight if it can.
Stars are small explosions switching on.
    Sometimes the heart is broken,
    sometimes it's a stone.

Under the Table

Secondly, I took refuge under the table,
her voice still storming, still swelling
after me, until I was snug
in the under-quiet, the solid
legs castling me.
Then her voice, closer, softening
to *Sorry*, to *Where are you?*
So I called her to me
and she came, peering under
as I edged over to make room.

Next, we were children
with the space of the floor between us,
the table grown huge.
She placed a bottle to spin
for kisses. We took turns.
But always it stopped sideways on.
What does this mean? I asked.
It means you may kiss my cheek.
So that's what I did.

I couldn't change the bottle's mind
no matter how many times
it was spun it played it safe.
Then she took up a pillow
a blanket, lay down, curled into sleep.

Later, she woke and said we must crawl
back into the world.
Now she sits across the table from me
not meeting my eyes.
Until she does:
which is when she bursts into laughter;
which is when I do too.

But first, I remember,
she had me cornered on the settee,
her anger like a car crash happening.
It felt like there could be blood; the possibility
that something would be broken.

Now That It's Happened

Now that it's happened, now that you've left yourself,
emptied the wardrobe of your clothes, emptied drawers;
        now that you've heaved your cases and a rucksack
onto a bus as the sun cracked through the shell of the day,
the street of shops and the small flats above still deep
in their dreams;
                now you've abandoned yourself
to the surprise of your absence in the morning—
a single bed with its blankets tucked under the chin
of the pillow, still holding some warmth, a cocoon
that has not yet learned it is empty;
                                now it has finally
happened, will you even imagine going out and looking
for yourself, perhaps some small half-hearted attempt
to call people you know, ask after yourself,
                                or will you
just accept it— not unexpected, not undeserved—let
yourself fade from your mind, the way others have?

Last Confession

After the catastrophe, it snowed indoors.
We rose on shaky legs to its first flurries.
Soon we stood on a bleached carpet, wore white
epaulets. The large rubber plant by the TV
thought it was Christmas. The lamp by the side
of my favourite chair wore a white hat. Next
we were ankle deep. A drift had built up
under the window. I scrunched over to the door,
cut an arc through innocence. I thought
to step into the hall, but if anything
the fall was heavier there. I looked across
at the coat rack, snow sculpture, Elgin Marbles.
One coat was slouched on the floor, its arms
up behind it like wings. An angel. Fallen.
I turned back into the room. My wife was down
on her knees looking up at the continuing fall,
manna from heaven, the solid ceiling keeping
nothing out; looking up as if she could see
the face of god as snow shrouded her.
I thought about trying to make it outside
but the windows were dark, hell frozen over.
The stairs up to the bedroom was an avalanche
waiting. *It's the Awakening*, my wife said,
arms out, a blonde crucifix. That was an hour ago.
Now I'm on top of the bookcase, the cat
beside me, hearing my last confession,
everything else is drowned, the snow a soft sea
rising. I am praying that the cat comes up
with something soon. I'm thinking of jumping.

That Young One

i. That Young One Has a Strange Head

on her, the Dark Father said when he heard
what she'd been doing. She was silent,
standing before the Dark Mother
with her hair and clothes dripping
as the Dark Mother fussed over her with a towel.
Who else would stand out in the yard
in the pelting rain, unmoving for an hour?
the Dark Father asked. No one answered.
The Dark Father never expected answers.
She is not of my blood! he said finally.
She hoped this would be enough
for him, that he would not beat her later.
The Dark Mother asked no questions.
But even if she did, how could That Young One
answer? No one would understand
that she'd been waiting for a door to open
in the rain, that she might step through.

ii. That Young One Always Leaves the Road

on her way to school so she may cross the field
with the clump of bushes in its centre.

The Dark Mother told her that the clump is a fairy fort
and if the farmer were to cut it down,

all of his animals would get sick and die.
If she has the time, That Young One stops at the clump

to examine the ground. She looks for footprints
leading in, where there are none leading out.

But the ground is too dry. In winter, she thinks
when there is frost or snow, she will find her path.

iii. The Dark Father Asks a Question

of the Dark Mother. It is a question
he has asked many times before.
As usual, it goes unanswered.
The Dark Mother pours strong tea
into a mug and heaps in sweetness.
She brings it to the Dark Father
with a smile. He takes the mug in one
hand and reaches up with the other
to touch the hand that the Dark Mother
places on his shoulder. That Young One
watches from behind the stair banisters
as the Dark Mother brings her head
down to the Dark Father's, her black hair
spilling across his black hair.
That Young One brings her own hand up
to brush her copper fringe from her eyes.

iv. That Young One Finds a Way

to punish the children who annoy her,
who steal her lunch, write on her books.

She takes the time to print the name
of the child in the new letters she is just

beginning to learn on a piece of paper
which she then folds three times.

With the folded name under her pillow,
she will dream of her revenge.

If she dreams of water, she will float
the paper in the well next morning.

If she dreams of a storm, she will flitter
it into the wind. When the child

who is named slips into a ditch on
the way to school or is blown home again

by a ravaging flu, That Young One
is not surprised. Nothing really bad

has ever happened. But That Young One
knows there is much she has to learn.

v. One Morning She Witnesses the Bright Father

hiding within the clump as she approaches it.
She sees him but pretends she doesn't.
She walks past slowly without glancing in

or turning around. His eyes, That Young One knows,
are following her as she finishes her crossing,
as she climbs the five-bar gate to reach the road.

She can feel him watching as she lifts her leg
over the top bar, pulling her skirt up
so it won't snag. The Dark Mother has told her

she despairs at the state of That Young One's
clothes. So That Young One tries to be careful.
The Bright Father stays in her mind all day at school.

She can feel his breath on the back of her neck
and, if she is very still, That Young One can feel
his finger stroke the tail of her spine.

vi. That Young One Worries She'll Forget

the brightness of her beginning.
As the evenings close in and
the dark sky floats down
into the fields, That Young One
tries to remember the white halls
she's sure she came from, the high
lamps mirrored in the glass floors.
She is getting heavy with years.
Only this morning, the Dark Mother
reminded her that in two week's time
she will be six years old. Yesterday
she found a doll that she used to
play with when she was little.
She had forgotten it. That Young One
worries about how easy it is
to forget. The Dark Father, she knows
forgets all the time. He makes promises
he never keeps, threats he seldom fulfills.

vii. She Sees the Bright Mother Crying

beside the five-bar gate as she crosses
to it. The Bright Mother sees her coming
and turns to leave before That Young One
comes upon her. *Wait*, That Young One
calls and the Bright Mother waits.
That Young One climbs the gate and sits
on the top bar, her feet tucked under
the second from top bar, to keep herself
steady. She is so close to the Bright Mother
that she can see her breath misting
the winter air. The Bright Mother
has stopped crying and is regarding
That Young One intently. *Do you know
how to get home?* That Young One asks.

No, the Bright Mother says. That Young One
takes the Bright Mother's face between
her hands and kisses her forehead.
She notices that the Bright Mother's red hair
is unwashed, that she smells, that her clothes
are ragged. *There will be a way,* she tells
the Bright Mother as she hops down
from the gate and heads off for school.

viii. The Dark Father Tells a Story

about the fairy folk.
He says that sometimes the fairies
fall in love with a human baby
and come to steal it.
But the fairies are not allowed
to just take the baby.
They must replace it
with one of their own,
a changeling. That Young One
watches as the dark-haired baby
is lifted from its cot,
its dark mother sleeping.
She can feel the copper-haired infant
being placed into the warm hollow
of those blankets, light
leaving the bedroom
as the Bright Father goes away
with his prize, leaves his cast-away baby.
What use is a changeling?
asks the Dark Father finishing his story.
There is no answer. That Young One
watches as the Dark Father stands,
turns, and walks from the room.
From a chair under the window,
the Dark Mother looks across at her.
The Dark Mother does not speak.

ix. That Young One Watches the Dark Mother

as she cuts her hair.
The Dark Mother snips at her hair
with a large pair of scissors ,
her face intent in the window glass.
Lock by lock, the Dark Mother's hair falls
to the floor. When she is finished,
the Dark Mother flicks back
the new length of her hair, her white neck
flashing into view for a moment.
When the Dark Mother goes off
to find the broom, The Young One
scoops up a portion of hair
and takes it to her bedroom.
She places the hair in a shoebox
she keeps under her bed,
carefully tucking it in
beside the pink ribbon, the knitted bootee,
the silver spoon the Dark Mother
had kept hidden
in the back of her wardrobe.

x. There Are Blue Lights Flashing

in the field and That Young One hurries.
She imagines a double door. Open.
She imagines bright people dancing. She thinks
she can hear music, like wind and leaves
and the high call of birds.

Last night she dreamt that there had been a bright light.
She had felt herself lifted from her bed.
But when she woke, it was the same dark room.

When That Young One tries to cross the field,
a policeman stops her. *Use the road*, he says.
There's a police car by the clump.
They are pulling the Bright Father out.

It's not safe here for little girls, the policeman says,
pushing her back to the road.

But the Bright Father has seen her.
She carries his face with her to into school.
It is dark and full of hate. It is as if the Bright Father
has put on someone else's face.
She has no one she can tell about this.

xi. Are You Looking for Me?

That Young One asks the Bright Mother
when she meets her on the road home from school.
No, the Bright Mother says, afraid.
That Young One notices that the Bright Mother
is wearing an extra coat. It is stained
as if the Bright Mother has been lying on the ground.
I'm not looking for anyone, the Bright Mother says,
not even myself. The Bright Mother is lost
That Young One decides and
She tries to tell her about the clump,
about the Bright Father's anger.
The Bright Mother doesn't want to listen.
The Bright Mother just wants to walk away.
Which she does.

The wind is freezing. That Young One feels it nipping
the backs of her knees as she goes home.
The Dark Mother has made soup for her.
Do you want me to stay here? she asks the Dark Mother.
If I could, I would keep you forever, the Dark Mother says.
The Dark Mother doesn't normally say this many words
so That Young One believes her.
The Dark Mother rises and goes to the dresser.
She picks up a red button and gives it to That Young One.
Heart-red, That Young One thinks,
taking it into her hands. The button is almost
big enough to cover the whole of her palm.

It is bright and glassy. There are four round holes
in the centre for thread. That Young One
takes the button to her room.
She puts it into her box to keep it safe.

xii. That Young One is Sweeping the Floor

when the Dark Father comes in. This
is something new and he stops to watch her.

That Young One has decided to make the place brighter.
She looks back at the Dark Father.

She looks a long way into his eyes.
He is tired, exhausted. His hands are dirty.

The Dark Father smiles.
She'll do, he tells the Dark Mother.

That Young One can see the way light enters
when the Dark Father smiles

and so, she smiles too. This is also something new.
We'll keep That Young One, the Dark Father says.

Lazarus Leaving

Lazarus Leaving

Pushing out of dark he sees the world again.
Trees climb into the sky, their limbs a burst of green
as they reach for the sun;
the sky an eternity of blue.

He stands whole in his wrapping sheets,
the smell of death still sickly-sweet in their folds, and he knows.
He knows he was gone and has come back,
that he was not and is now again.

Wonder fills him but then empties.
The fruit of death cannot be un-eaten.
His eyes he thinks, if he looked in a mirror, would be stark,
might kindle a terror. He shakes out his stiffness,

thinks of his wife, his children, waking
into their grief, getting used to his absence, remaking
the rooms of the house—the breakfast table,
the evening cluster of chairs—to a shape that excludes him.

He turns his back on the town, knows as he leaves
there are no second chances,
he will be haunted by his own death,
wonders who played this trick on him and why.

Digging

She comes back to me.
It's as if a gauze curtain is pulled aside
and a snatch of my dream
sits there looking at me –
questioning eyes, her pelt
grey in the shadow of that place,
but fox nonetheless. She sits
still as a moment of fear.

I try to bring back the rest,
want her moving, picture her
white-tipped brush like a flame –
as if imagining is the same as dream.
It is not. I dig through my mind, dig.
But all I find is this one image.

Her eyes are serious, a sort of
do-not-dare-forget solemnity.
And I have forgotten. Now, when
I look, there she is looking back
as if she will always sit there
watching me at my useless
digging, as if I am making
a final place to lie down.

Jinn

A Jinn, she said when I told her
about that pull on my shirt
that turned me to face empty space.

Moments earlier, I thought I'd heard
my name called, so this was
someone catching up with me.

My mouth had got itself ready
to smile, to say *Hi*, almost did,
though no one was there.

Perhaps I imagined it.
An hallucination, my son said
and meant it. But I know what I felt –

my shirt tightened at the front,
as I was pulled up short
by the jerk of fabric at the back.

I had to straighten myself out
before I could move on.

All Souls' Night

Three saucers placed on a platter,
one's filled with clay, one holds a ring,
the third is brimming water.

All soul's night: the membrane
between the worlds in tatters, a wing
of darkness brushes past your skin.

The future cold and wide as an ocean,
the past just something that you sling
on your back and take along. The notion

of swimming pulls at you as friends fasten
a cloth across your eyes, tie with string,
then spin you, place you in position.

Now you must choose your future blind
by reaching out. Touching wetness will fling
you on a journey, an emigrant; find

the ring and you will marry within
a year; but bury your fingers and they'll sing
at your wake before next Halloween.

The Voices of the Dead

I sit with a coffee and my dead brother.
There was a time when he was older than I.
Now he's so young. We reminisce about Christmases –

the real pine trees, the fairy lights, the way daddy
always read Dickens for us each Christmas Eve, and how
maybe that's what got me writing. I remember for us

the open fires daddy would build, the way he twisted
newspaper into ropes and knotted them, the way
he gently placed the firewood over and then the coal

on top, how the paper coils reddened as the flame
from his match honeycombed in, the sticks snapping
and barking. He would hold an opened newspaper

over the mouth of the fireplace, force it to breathe
through the teeth of its grate. When he took it away
the fire always sat there, contented, the coals settling

into their nest, the flames opening and closing
their beaks. We expect the dead to be wise but they are
only themselves. *What did you expect?* he says.

You don't think of me that often any more. True.
Life does that. It fills you up with its noise,
leaves little space in your head for the voices of the dead.

Words are Less than Half the Story

When my grandmother died
we waked her in a funeral parlour.
The window curtains were closed
but the busy street still happened.
She had been dead a day yet
sometime that afternoon I felt her go.
It was as if the fabric of the room's
air had been plucked, an almost
popping sound, the way the ears reset
themselves when a plane lands.

Death can be so casual. It can happen
in schools or pubs, nightclubs,
restaurants, on planes and buses or
sometimes, carelessly, at checkpoints,
the back seats of police cars. It can be
furiously precise from a rooftop
half a mile away. Or it can call you
by your first name, the way your mother
might have called you in from the street
and might tell you to wipe your feet,
wash your hands, before sitting down.

I did not feel my father go. A phone
call told me. He wasn't there when
I went home. I'm not sure I was either.
Despite being crowded, the church too
felt empty. But I knew the real weight
of his absence when we carried his coffin
out into light, raindrops calling from leaves,
the mounded earth darkened, wet.

We think of death as someplace
else. But it is no place. We will never
know it has happened because it is not
something that happens. It is something
that stops us happening. I'm haunted
by the idea of future generations,
those not yet born but who are here
all the same, peering at me, wondering
who I am; how my mind works; how I can
possibly live in these barbarous times.

Late into London Blues

I land in London late and in the rain,
fly into Gatwick airport in the rain,
the darkening sky spreading like a stain.

My pickup calls, says he's an hour away,
the traffic's bad, he's still an hour away,
it's like a cortège on the motorway.

The cars outside the terminal look tired.
All the rain and wind-lashed cars are tired.
The sky's unbalanced, the evening high-wired.

In the nearby Premier Inn I sit and wait,
I sit down with a coffee and I wait.
The weather and my mood won't separate.

I strain into the dark but nothing fits.
The world is like that now: nothing fits.
Our dumbed-down world is missing most its bits.

I need to join the edges of my journey,
join the broken edges of my journey,
but everything's now make-do or make-easy.

Time's a pulsing river on my wrist.
My life is bleeding slowly on my wrist,
just ticking to a place where nothing's first.

My home is waiting, arms about itself,
an empty house, its arms about itself,
and in the garden night stalks like a thief.

And even as I wait, my house grows old.
We'll not recognize each other, being so old;
my heart stuttering inwards, its breath gone cold.

I flew back to London in the rain.
An old man home to England in the rain,
now sat down, might not stand up again.

The North

You can go too far north,
the rain skittering off the windscreen,
your headlights doused by dark.

You might think to get out
and walk under that hunched-over sky,
the roadside trees leaning towards you

as if ready to uproot and run.
There are mountains beyond the grey,
granite-hard and headstrong,

harbourers of old hatreds, sharp-cragged
like the accents of its people,
un-giving, suspicious.

And beyond that, the sea
clawing up the rock-face, bone-hungry,
berserker, ripping out of the night,

its death-song howling.
Do not. Turn around.
Let nothing be said. Go back

to your old age,
your weariness. Let the north
come find you in your bed.

Dancing with the Dead

I would be buried with my smart phone
fully charged and placed within
my stiffing fingers. I want the chance
of a little light in all that dark.

In the south of Ireland there's an odd
tradition which has gravediggers
descend into the grave before
they shovel in the dirt.

They loosen the screws on the lid,
as if leaving the door unlocked and
easy to open on the Last Day.

In Madagascar they take the wrapped
mummies of their ancestors
out of their tombs and dance with them
every seven years, unwrapping them
into the now, introducing them
to their recent relatives.

I would use my placed mobile, to keep up
with social media, check how easily
I might have been forgotten.

My nephew-in-law's Facebook Wall
still receives messages
years after he's been grounded—
Missing you big time, Buddy.
I was notified: *Dara Delargey and
11 other friends have their birth-
day today*, 2 years after he'd stopped aging.

I want the alarm set on my phone
to wake me, to startle passers by –
a bell in an old Victorian graveyard, the end
of its string being pulled
by a hand in a box six feet under.

And I could text you, say *hi*,
say *How's your day?* ask
What's it like now amongst the living?

Wind

Wind comes gushing out of a gate
in the side of the sky. You are blown back
by the current. It would release you
from this place. You are fighting
pure force. If you are not to be swept away
you must find something more rooted
than yourself. Even your voice
is snatched from your mouth, your skin
wants to peel from your skull.
You lie flat, you bury your head
in your hands, think down,
think hole in the ground, think maybe
this is the wind you've been expecting
all of your life, the one that's been waiting
for you here in the future like a dog
locked out at night. Well night has come
and the dog will have its bone.

Beannacht

Prayer for Ramadan

For Z

If you can bear the weight
of so much lightness,
may your body be a knife
paring away slivers
of appetite.

There are places inside
that only echo when empty.
Sound yourself out. Want.
Let night come like a prayer
answered.

Let your table be burdened
with nothing but its own shape.
Let your cup wait a moon-beat
for the sun to sleep
before spilling over.

When night falls
may the faces of your family,
those here, those elsewhere,
be your joy, and
may love come upon you
in all of its names.

Love Poem for Oreo

Released, she bolts for cover in my over furnished
apartment. I'm minding her for eight days.
It's evening. I leave her be, have a small supper.
Now, nothing. I could be alone. I call her
but she's not so easily tricked. An hour. I call again.
She must want to be found. She comes crying, tentative,
trigger-sensitive. I remember that level of anxiety,
being sick with it. She lets me stroke her just enough
to calm things down, then eases away,
smells her way around her changed world.

> My business totters,falls
> in the Crash. I put in everything
> I have left to get it standing.
> But it will not climb to its feet.
> All is lost. I squeeze what furniture
> I can from my house into this
> rented apartment, walk daily
> from room to room. To be still
> is to be sick. The past
> will not let the future enter.

It's next morning. I check her food bowls.
She's eaten little, has parked herself under
the TV cupboard. I crouch into her headlights,
call her out. She comes, wants attention, circles
me as I sit, brushes against me. When I begin
to stroke her, she switches on her little engine.

> I'm alone with a voice
> asking the same questions.
> This is not a time of answers.
> How will I provide now
> for our old age? People call me
> looking for money. I wonder
> if I'll hold steady in a job interview.
> The idea of putting on a suit,
> a tie, and going out, is too much.

She comes to find me, finds me reading.
I lean down, rub her head, her neck, her white bib,
go back to my book. She calls, her big eyes
opening my heart when I look down. I make room and
she leaps onto the armchair, steps onto my lap,
walks her front paws up my body, brings her face
close to mine. For some reason I expect her
to kiss me. But she turns, settles on the wide
armrest, holds herself there like a sphinx.

      Each morning the whole weight
      of the room must be lifted
      to get out of bed. I try
      to plan something positive—
      a call home, a cheap breakfast
      out, a meeting to talk about
      a meeting about a talk about
      a job. My main regret is not
      being able to retire early, to have
      real time to write. Then the answer
      arrives. Just pick up a pen.

I've been out. When I settle into my armchair
she climbs onto my lap, stares into my face
as if she can read there the passing of time.
Do I look old? I ask her. But she is indifferent.
Time probably means something else to her. She might
think I'm crazy. She steps onto the cluttered table
beside me, moves carefully, delicately, a ninja. You wouldn't
know she was moving. She occupies silence like an expert.

There is a new balance now.
I rise early to write—
before phone, before emails.
Just me and a coffee.
There is a new job to go out to
later. There is still toil.
There is still a way
of living in the world.

Now the quality of silence is different. It is
an empty silence, one that confirms she has left me.
It would never have worked out anyway—
the language barrier, the age difference, religion,
species, politics. She could have texted me, sent
a selfie, left a paw-print in the margin.
But she's reminded me of something about time—
you can live through it, you get to go home.

Apple

She calls me out of the blue
and the sun startles awake.

She is happy.
I feel it like a breeze.

I am eating an apple, the outer skin
bruised but the flesh still fair.

She says, *I've bought you a coffee*
and sends a picture.

The coffee is lidded in a paper cup.
An orchestra tunes up in my head

and my heart is humming.
I imagine her opening out her wings;

the brilliance, the purity. She is saying
something else but the words

have turned into notes. It must still
be morning but I've lost track—just

this brightness, the breeze, her
in full flight, me tossing the apple core

directly into the waste bin
on the first attempt.

Weight

For Holly, 5 weeks old

The world is loaded with terror, a cocked weight
of loss in so many hearts. This is the force
of our days. It masses close as a border, a restaurant.
We are burdened by gods we have let loose. Fear
heavy-hands us, its bulk blocking all doors.

But there is a new weight in my world,
a small warm weight here on my chest.
Her tummy pushes against my tummy
with every breath she takes: fast, gulping in
the world. Her knees are up high like a jockey's.
Her arms are wide against my ribs.
She is rushing into her life at a gallop, the whole field
of it, the wide plain of it, in front of her.

There is a new weight in my world.
The force of it outweighs all that is wrong,
all that is broken. I have a granddaughter.
She is perfect. She is the exact weight of love.

Night after Night

For Lynsey—Feb 2017

Fitful nights—she wakes you; wants.
Sleep drags at your shoulders as you go to her.
Night after night. Drugged

with weariness. The hint now of a pretty girl
behind her baby face. How quickly
love surfaces when the future shows itself

like this. For the future is full of partings.
So many faces will bloom, then fall away.
So many songs will rise from the swollen heart.

Remembering your Green Dress

For Z, Dubai, Oct 2014

I sit watching the sea,
the way it gathers itself, its energy swelling
before its mad dash in,
the whole fizz and plash of it,
rushing close.

I picture you in that green dress
that danced you younger.

The sky is losing itself a little,
becoming sleepy-eyed, hazy.
Some days it is hard to hold onto yourself.

I am not sure when I first felt old.
But more and more I am reminded
that an old man waits for me
in a mirror.

You are not Lebanese, you said.
The thought having come to you,
you phoned me to voice it.

The sea gathers back into itself.

What I mean is, you are not from this region,
so some day you will have to go.
And I said *Yes, some day I will go.*

The waves flash back in, slapping at the beach.
There are Russian girls out in the water.
The sun smiles on them.
They seem newly burned into womanhood.

Some moments can last longer than others.

You turned—a small swirl, a slight lift of green—
to show the plunging back of your dress,
the audacity of it,
the girlish wish of it.

You are the daughter I never had,
one I have found
here in the Middle East.

The horizon has returned,
the sky reasserts itself.

An old woman,
whose breasts spill as she scoops
something small from the sand, is young again.
I can see youth traced in her movements,
see it linger a while as she forgets
and stands to watch the Russian girls
jump into the waves.

What shall I do, you ask,
what shall I do when you're gone?

The sea has never known how to be still.
Ah, but the magnificence of it,
so filled up with itself that it sings.
Love is like that:
it cannot be contained.

At the Gym

Two girls, fourteen or fifteen years old,
in the almost empty gym, are coaching
each other in stretching exercises
they've seen in magazines and they're making
a pig's ear of it. They lift my morning
all the same, with their cute cluelessness,
their gangly limbs, their gawky movement.

But there's a lesson here too:
things need not always be done correctly,
they mostly need to be enjoyed. We should be free
to be out of tune and to accompany ourselves
by plonking arbitrary notes on a piano.

What joy then when a key struck and a wrong
note sung, harmonise. Here are the girls
lying on their sides, lifting their legs
into the pale morning light, telling each other
This is one of the best ways to lose weight,
and not a spare ounce between them.

Hands

Ibn Battua Mall, 2015

My hand is taken
by a small warm hand —
a girl, maybe four years old, gold skin,
hair a scatter of black. She tugs
or maybe it's that I hold back enough
for her to know her mistake.

She takes her hand away,
regards me like a question —
her brown eyes serious.
She scans the crowd, runs to a man
some steps away, his mind gone
ahead of his body.

She takes his hanging hand
and anchors him. He looks at her
then lets his mind go free again.
She glances back, solemn,
centred, minding him.
And then she smiles: brightness.

I hold the moment close,
a state of grace.

Ghazal: Marie

All summer I've been old, nothing's new, Marie,
when there's only myself. It's all the same sound & hue, Marie.

Back in the day, we would play hide & seek
and I would come searching each nook for you, Marie.

But my journey has taken us into the heat
of this Dubai summer—too much for you, you withdrew, Marie.

So we talk now on *FaceTime* and phone, meet
on the airways, the net. What else can we do, Marie,

we're stuck with my work? But here I can reap
enough for an end that befits what I sow, Marie.

Look, summer is now cooling its feet
in the ocean, the breezes are blue. It's time to renew, Marie.

Now you tell me that you're booking your flight.
It'll be a relief, let me tell you, to return to being two, Marie.

So when you disembark and call *Frank* in your bright
clear voice, I'll be the one edging up to you in the queue, Marie.

Beannacht

For Marie, in celebration of 40 years of marriage.

May your days keep pace with you
and not run on ahead.
May you always know what you're about.
May all doors find a way
to let you out.

May the voice in your head find comfort
in the work of your hand.
May quiet enter you gently,
the way the edge of an ocean
lips at the land.

May you never fear the coming night,
the dark-driven.
May you rest into it like a pilgrim
returning home,
heart-lightened, heart-shriven.

May life find a way to laugh at you
such that you may laugh
at yourself,
laugh until your heart breaks,
doing nothing by half.

May flowers turn their heads
when you pass. May the birds
know your name.
May your pen never run out of ink.
May your heart be the same.

Notes

Holding Your Tongue

Mo ghrá gheal — My bright love
A ghrá mo chroi — Love of my heart
Gaeltacht — native Gaelic speaking parts of Ireland;
tigín — small house, cabin
Dineen — One of the great lexicographical works in Irish is the dictionary first published by An tAthair Pádraig Ó Duinnín (also known as Patrick Dineen) in the year 1904 and expanded in 1927. It was an Irish — English dictionary. This dictionary is still used today on account of the richness of its content.

Promenade des Anglais

This is a 7km promenade along the Mediterranean at Nice, France. On 14 July 2016, a truck was deliberately driven at revellers celebrating Bastille Day on the Promenade. The driver, 31-year-old Mohamed Lahouaiej-Bouhlel, also shot at others. The vehicle was surrounded by police near the Palais de la Méditerranée, and Bouhlel was shot dead. 84 were killed, and many others injured. Two people later died, bringing the total who died to 86.

Only the Rain

amadán — fool — Irish

Aisling: Beirut

Aisling: Irish for "dream." The aisling (pronounced "ashling") is a vision or dream poem, which developed in Gaelic poetry in Munster during the late seventeenth and eighteenth centuries. It has its origins in the Old French reverdie, which celebrates the arrival of spring, often in the form of a beautiful woman.

That Young One

The story of this sequence is built around the idea of a changeling—where a human baby is stolen and a fairy child left in its place. It also plays with the idea that fairies lived in bright underground halls beneath fairy rings (naturally occurring circles in woods or grasslands) and were themselves bright to look at. The sequence is told from the point of view of a young girl who believes that she is a changeling.

Dancing With the Dead

The practice of dancing with the dead in Madagascar is called *Famadihana*.

Beannacht

Beannacht—Blessing—Irish

www.ingramcontent.com/pod-product-compliance
Lightning Source LLC
LaVergne TN
LVHW041202080426
835511LV00006B/708